T0208059

# OF LIFE REVIEWED

# OF LIFE REVIEWED

Philosophy in Flight on the Wings of Poetry

## WALTER SLACK

# OF LIFE REVIEWED
## PHILOSOPHY IN FLIGHT ON THE WINGS OF POETRY

iUniverse books may be ordered through booksellers or by contacting:

iUniverse
1663 Liberty Drive
Bloomington, IN 47403
www.iuniverse.com
1-800-Authors (1-800-288-4677)

Because of the dynamic nature of the Internet, any web addresses or links contained in this book may have changed since publication and may no longer be valid. The views expressed in this work are solely those of the author and do not necessarily reflect the views of the publisher, and the publisher hereby disclaims any responsibility for them.

Any people depicted in stock imagery provided by Thinkstock are models, and such images are being used for illustrative purposes only.
Certain stock imagery © Thinkstock.

ISBN: 978-1-4917-7223-2 (sc)
ISBN: 978-1-4917-7222-5 (e)

Library of Congress Control Number: 2015910838

Print information available on the last page.

iUniverse rev. date:  10/13/2015

# CONTENTS

In
Memory
Of
ALISON BROTT
1958 - 1965
She was a joy
To Those
Who Knew and Loved Her

# INTRODUCTION

It is necessary for the poet to examine life, strip it bare of superficial elements, if he is to ply his craft with the depth and meaning that are his responsibility and if he is to claim any merit at all for his verses. Poetry is the medium of the soul, the heart, but it ought also appeal to the mind. Verse fails in one important aspect if it does not at times afford the intellect a certain species of enjoyment and stimulation to further thought. Such is the aim and hope of the poetry contained within these pages.

The poetry offered here attempts an integration of process theology and ethical humanism. It seeks to deal with the nature of the universe and our relationship to that universe, as we move in the realms of things and of persons. God is treated here with all the joy, abandon, precision and limitations which poetry permit. A humble effort is made to define deity as modern science and new theological thinking have afforded us the tools to do. This application of process theology represents something of a break with conventional modes of thought about God, but then, we live in an era of theological flux symbolized by the "God is Dead" movement. Revised and refined thinking about God and our relationship to ultimate reality is needed by modern people— both in prose and poetic forms—if we are to achieve a heightened understanding of the world in which we subsist.

Poetry does not admit of proof, though it does evince a conviction of the emotions not always available to poor, dead prose. A more systematic verification of the author's views expressed here must be found in his other, less poetic works. Here the aim has been to present in one form of expression a philosophy of life. At times the poetry herein speaks the sublime language of theology; at other times it utters the hard, blunt voice of mill hands and coal miners. In the latter, it seeks not to shock, but rather to convey the realness and humanity of ordinary people. The poetry which only sings of springtimes and sunsets misses much of the zest, meaning, and tragedy of the human condition. Humans are beings evolving in an environment of capabilities and liabilities. Poetry can have little merit if it does not strive to portray us in our real situations of loving, suffering, enjoying, fighting and dying.

# GOD

What call you God—artificer, sorcerer?
An ill-used cognomen for the follies of men,
Fabled nursery of human brotherhood—
Working a deception on the author of the deed,
For *what* fraternity that doth prevail
Issues from the clay-formed hands of man.
Love is a vessel turned by a humbler wheel
Than that vast orb which is the compass of God.
Men curse the gods that let them be—
An imputed necessity to solace their cares.
How dim their sight to volition's command!
What imposition there be, staining their genesis,
Is accusation of a far less divine intention.
God is a matrix of Time and Space—
Order and extension, autonomy and diversity,
Assigning dimension, while bereft of decision.
It is a universality of the sublime and commonplace;
An ordering of substance forming man and star,
Eternal, yet subject *and* sovereign of Time.
Artisan of Matter made complex and unique,
Whose Being finds identity in each revelation.
God is *not* an empty Form, the essence of essences,
Void of all amplitude, save sterile perfection—
Cold in its static ring of immobility.
For God is pulse, change, and unfoldment;
A dark fount unknown even to Itself,
Harboring the materials of Present and Future—
An unshaped stuff, measurable by none,
Framed by God and Man to diversity's norm.
God is movement, surging and restless,
Bursting with a creativity, new with each moment,
Replenished by an order which knows no denouement;
Measure and direction, fermented by opportunity—
A *possibility* as vast as the womb of Time.

1

Man within this universal process stands,
The child of order and chance created.
His countenance and stance, grubbed from the earth;
Foul clay—the holy benediction of God.
Man and star a system made divine.
The star a beacon of regularity supreme—
Hearth for life—peripatetic partner.
Man the slime of some primeval sea,
*Itself* the consequence of accident and symmetry.
This human mire—Oh, inauspicious mud,
From your loins has noble Reason sprung.
We act and by our thought reveal
The variation within our being etched.
Nobility confounds barbarity unleashed.
We move within the bosom of God's potentiality;
Limited things—tools of uglier passions,
Yet authors of the Church, the Poem, the Dream.
This then is God: system and difference;
Each by a holy choice made whole—
Natures so unlike, yet the spring of unity.

# BEING

Some primordial stuff through us oozes with nameless insistence;
It hinges thing to thing, cementing joint, adhering and dividing.
From its formless ground diverse natures shape and kindle;
Things in profusion grow, cut from its blameless trunk providing.

Trite vessels of common habit draw name from its inclusion;
Tools of familiar lot fashion from its mound of eternal nurture.
What we be, particular fragments in a sea of multiplicity,
From Being is brought to pass, relentless logic to adjure.

Singular things evolve, vast effusion of an unknown spring—
Silent witness to creation, solitary thought and deed so stamp—
Each mortal thing a *span* of potential, realizing its fulfillment.
This stuff, Mother of Earth, binds infinity by an ethereal clamp.

Oh, boundless substance, core of God, pervade my heart and soul,
Impute a lofty lineage for a husk, plain wrapper to behold—
Sprung from the source of Being, invading the last ramparts of space.
Did the gentle Buddha divine you in his Way—Eight-Fold?

A sea of Being by God produced—restless tension of creation—
His Nature a vast immensity, unfolding in material garb,
Seeking for knowledge concealed in dark recesses of unknown rectitude—
The extension of things flung to the world as a divine barb.

God *must* fashion Himself from the ready masonry of complex Being,
Else nought His inner soul—senseless save by Matter known.
An article of Being enhances divine perception, Himself reveal—
Panoply of power, panorama of universe, a holy necessity shown.

Knowledge of Self for God a path, His own visage to discover;
God and world a stream, flowing onward to eternal learning.
The shape of things the form of God, voice to His inmost parts,
Invoking a creation of a flow of Being, lovingly *outward* yearning.

# TIME

Time's fleeting step imprint
Subtle etchings of an endless tide,
Thus made fine by a delicate cut—
Moment by moment—eternity to mark.

Time is the pulse beat of God—
Secret rhythm of His inner extension,
Ceaseless stream immersing creation—
No beginning *or* end divided.

Time *is* God—dimension divine—
Locking Matter in the grip of Change.
Moving process eroding hindrance;
Forming anew *His* pervading Self.

God and Earth would static lie,
If Time cease its relentless beat—
Urging, ordering to its count—
A plentitude of Being made aware.

Youth and Age for Time a mask
Veiling the permanent, onward rush,
Of God's step by step unfolding,
Affording direction to *His* fulfillment.

Oh, girdle of Space, Time is master
Arranging Matter to its own command.
Time and Space blend as one
Shaping things on their wayward march.

Time is a chain, uniting events,
Cementing diversity in a single pattern.
All *and* nothing, imperceptible to view,
Save as its children change and erode.

Time is invisible, quiet worker;
Stern martinet, yet escaping inquiry.
Time is *relation* of things in motion
Issuing from Matter, throbbing linked.

Here no chattel indentured to clocks;
Watches and such trap not its flight.
Time is freedom, winged splendor,
Sovereign of Earth, instructing God.

# NATURE

The world is a pulse of vitality,
Of Life throbbing in hearts
Called into being by desire
To live in the sun of tomorrow.

Nature is a mystic chorus—
A billion throats demanding
A share of each new moment—
A right to grow and decay.

Nature is law and process,
Of stone and tree and beast
Sharing a common beginning
In the fiery belly of a star.

Matter is our mutual contract—
Symbol of our marriage to earth—
Dust, the paste of generations—
Water, the ointment of life.

Oh, harsh is the call of Nature,
Its will our siren song.
We, but the mud of creation
Shaped by the laws inherent.

Billions labor in silence,
Nature's imperative to fill—
Completing their task by union
For Life is served by the womb.

Man, in his wisdom, ponders
His ties to Nature entwined-
His mind the effect of Necessity—
Tool for the wooing of earth.

Man is mired by his origin—
Plebeian mud of the ages,
Yet strong his claim to dominion,
Anointed by a surge of Reason.

# BEAUTY

What fragile hidden touch inspire
The common earth to shape anew,
Raising to beauty coarsest flesh—
A silken ornament of grace.

Beauty is symmetry carved by love,
Rubbed smooth by fancy's stone,
Polished in tender knowledge kept
Of rougher edge concealed within.

Bloom and vibrance enchant the eye,
Captivate the heart, yearning drawn.
Harmony imbues form and depth
With balance exalting spirit within.

Calm repose and kindled dream
My soul attracts, made alive,
Infuse my sense with purpose dim
Of secrets stored within the line.

I see and know, yet mute the tongue
What Nature, in her dominion holds
As gift to man, her dwelling probe
Of delicate pose carved for time.

Beauty stands inward pressed,
Waiting a soul, sensitive, akin,
Complete a union of world and will—
Now *one* for a moment of quiet rapture.

# MAPLE TREE

Thoughts on an autumn afternoon

---

On days of autumn's increasing grace,
I watch that maple tree aspire
To shed her vestiges of spring—
Her verdant pulse now sluggish from frost,
Her leaves a cascade of color soon devoured,
Consumed by a rhythm too old for time.
The maple stands as a diadem of life;
Soon entombed by the silence of snow,
Clothed so nobly as a wintry spire.
The maple yearns with her secrets deep,
Seeking a knowledge forever hers.
In her bough runs the sap of eternity,
Now surging with life come unexpected,
Serving a cause as a hostage of design.
Once more the rhythm will demand its due.
Beauty will fade and promise retreat.
The cold will crush until she would cry,
If Nature had given her sense to speak.
Pondering the mystery that within her lies.
Her life and mine a common yearning;
My mouth but a voice for her to speak,
Uttering of harshness and beauty shared—
Both the lineaments of an unknown God.
Our being, the fragment of a larger source.
I watch and write and hope to understand;
The maple yearns with a logic set within—
A part of dumb creation made divine,
Mine the biography of her growth and grief.
This tree is God writ small for me;

He no savior for my fancied sins.
This tree and I are but a common way
That God may find fulfillment of Himself,
A union of vitality made supreme.

# CLOUDS

One afternoon I chanced to scan
The sky beyond my window set.
The clouds before me softly ran,
Scurrying home before the wind.

Galleons made with billowy sail;
A great flotilla of eerie ships.
Their silent majesty did not pale—
Awesome power so loosely spent.

Tall barks upon the azure blue,
Tranquil in their wending way—
I would that I the sky might woo,
Their gentle secrets to pursue.

If I were granted one last boon,
I'd wish myself upon their decks,
And lull my soul with an airy tune,
As these great ships stood out to sea.

# LEAVES

Leaves boundless in autumn blow,
Helter-skelter, row on row.
Aimless in their headstrong flight,
Fearful of Nature's rushing might.

Vanity of spring hapless wanes;
Frost promises winter's pains.
Fugitives, fugitives fill the skies.
Have they heard that summer dies?

Pristine beauty now is spurned,
As useless husks they are burned.
Into the fires they hopeless went;
A fragrance to the heavens sent.

# WIND

The wind derives I know not where;
It touches gently on my face.
I search this wind for definition;
It only laughs and ripples on,
Nudging leaf and creaking bough.
Come follow me, it bids me on—
For yesterday was my mother;
Tomorrow a harbor of new repose.
The wind is a sprite, now dancing on,
Graceful, it comes and stirs the air,
Companion and friend, helpmate of man.
Soon it changes, brother of storm,
Lashing at man's frail earthenworks,
Framing demise of impudent man,
Who dares steal away from its awful wrath.
The winds are slave to flower and bird,
Imparting to each a service dear.
Upon its shoulders the flowers confer
A fragrance that is their heart dispelled.
The birds upon their mighty crests
Are borne aloft and soaring wheel.
Wind is a wanderer, laggard and soothing,
Moving elsewhere in relentless march.
It takes and gives, but answers not
Concerning the nature of its pedigree.
Vagabond, Vagabond, heedless fly,
Touch me softly—I ask not why.

# WINTER

Winter descends, cold hymn of perfection,
Chilling heart with stillness abrupt—
A pure mantle of snow hiding the scars—
Lesions of summer etched by storm.

Trees riven by cascades of ice,
Cracking limb with a frigid grip.
Boughs, denuded, bend in prayer—
Supplication for mercy unheeded.

Costumed for winter, marbled in ice,
Trees stand as sentinels mute
Guarding earth, awaiting spring's charge—
A sword and buckler of wind and snow.

Winter is severe, unfriendly in its wrath—
Giant clouds of snow unleashed,
Quieting the restless passions of summer,
Coupled with autumn's careless abandon.

Icy minstrel with a song of death,
Winter with her mission flies;
Work abounds, clearing the wreckage—
Remnants of season's glories past.

Life to be stripped to its naked core,
Scraped by the fingers of winter raw—
Make ready the earth for the onset of life,
World come alive with the sap of spring.

# LIFE

Life is lived; its energy spent—
Hordes conceived in evident lust.
Dawn to dusk the soil is scratched;
A deficient yield from an adamant earth.
Millions teem in forgotten wastes—
Life to Death and Death to Life.
An endless cycle—one vast deception?
Man *Meaning* inhere where waste abounds?
Is Life one yawning void of absurdity;
Dread sired by accident and fear?
Some sages, in their learning steeped,
Aver that man in estrangement is kept.
Anguish and fear a necessary key,
Unlocking perception of divine ambition.
As long as we walk in a want of Grace,
Meaning is denied and our efforts futile.
This Grace is sown with design intended;
A random few the harvest field.
Can this be life—a divine selection,
Where work and duty count for nought,
Save by a tyrant's unreasoning nod?
What *is* the indelible print of Life?
Into this world of scope uncharted,
Each man is by a force propelled,
Tying together muscle and brain—
Living tissue in an ornate gown.
In his freedom he is clothed,
Shorn of responsibility's chain.
Such is Man—the naked babe—
Man is the warden of his moral keep;
Framer of decalogues ever stern.
Morality doth freedom thus require,
To hone an edge on value's blade.
Freedom's not license—as Sartre avers;

Dismal source of emptiness compounded.
Freedom is man's badge of certitude,
Yet act it within a conspiring web.
Pleasure and pain—the hedonist's creed;
A polar star for man's navigation.
Bentham's Masters thus point the way,
Affording guidance for our wayward step.
Toddling babe and benighted savage,
The fiery poker both perceive—
A hostile source of searing flesh.
A second star of moral gravitation
Is Community shaping our formless stuff.
Burke and Rousseau its learned heralds;
We, as putty to this master builder.
Community is architect of all our dreams,
Fashioning us to its age-old norms,
Raising the unlettered to shared address—
A confraternity of value and tradition.
Man is thus from these poles suspended;
His values the product of piety and choice.
Here on the further marches of Meaning,
Man must his *only* life construct.
Masonry and timbers derived from custom;
Cement from pain and pleasure partaken.
Life is a mixture of purpose imputed—
Most deduced, but some decided,
As man upon his axis whirls.
Life is not a void abhorrent.
A mingling of freedom in chance revealed;
It remains for us to create the plot.
Meaning arises in love and friendship,
In selfless service to the helpless.
Germination of joy, a noble role.
Life is a pad upon which we write

Whatever memorial we care to leave.
Goodness may be the deep-cut word,
Or atrocity the degrading deed.
Meaning is there for those who seek,
If they but pause and attempt to read.

# BIRTH

From cosmic orb of unknown source
Her spark of life took fire.
Her kindling came of purest love,
Sieved through the clay of toil.

No gods within their hidden sphere
Could work a thing so fine,
As this young life of fragile weave
Now cast into our keep.

Thus are the elements so mixed in you,
That virtue will be served.
Etch deep within her secret stores
All your remembered grace.

Our lives are but a compass point,
To right her navigation.
Yet infinite her growing needs—
Oh, serve in stout compassion.

We give—and hope to fail her not—
This dross of human hope.
But are we made for more than that?
We *live* by her creation.

# PARENTS

The soil from which I spring was sweet,
Oh, ancient realm of callused folk—
Taciturn peasants mixed with the earth
Muscle and sweat to build a new land.
My mother's granite, strong and silent.
Her tight-lipped courage an inspiration,
Fount of strength, giving and forgiving—
Her heart a shelter from distress and hurt.
She asked precious little from life,
Guiding her children like a wary hen
Around pitfall and unsuspected trap—
Disciplining us with word or glance.
Frail of stature, devotion her pledge,
Service to offspring that we might grow
Secure in love and protection kept—
Too soon from the nest to test our wings.
My father's a man with foibles of flesh,
A molten temper and a ready response—
Limited vision, unschooled in the world,
Taught by experience—a rigorous teacher.
A rough hand and a humorous heart—
Skilled craftsman, childhood friend—
Wild in his youth with ladies and liquor—
Bootlegger, farmer, and wandering gypsy.
Human, so human, this breathing clay,
Virtue and vice so mixed with hardship—
Teaching of life with mistakes committed—
Nourishing me in my quest for learning.
Of stout materials were my parents made—
Courage and fear, love and anger—
With these they did my soul impress,
Shaping stuff to a human measure.

My life is theirs, a treasured gift,
Ignite my spark of growing flame.
Blood is a bond, entwining hearts—
A mutual love between us flows.

# CHILDREN

"Done with dining," he informs us;
"Fling the remnants to the wind."
"Call my men," he murmurs lightly;
"Who shall today my favor win?"

To the hall as the Lord awaits him
Strides Sir Matthew of Bath-us-More.
"Beckon him here," the Princeling utters;
"My stout companion of the candy war."

Brave Sir Matthew—a winsome knight;
Friend of the Prince and retainer bold.
Each a warrior of tested mettle,
Yet neither more than two years old!

Deep in converse; who can ponder,
What they say with sign and glance.
Words are shared, approval given;
Our young Prince demands his lance.

To the tourney field they scamper—
Tests of might and main to suffer.
A sporting joust upon a wager,
That's enough the match to spur.

Long the day they feint and parry,
Down the one and then the other,
Till at last our warriors weary;
Laugh they both and embrace the other.

Homeward trudge the weary warriors—
Tattered mail and broken crowns.
Gone the laughter shared in sporting;
Now we hear but muffled sounds.

Hard at play and now to slumber;
Another day its course has run.
To his chambers soft we bear him—
This young Prince who is our son.

# MAN

Can we but discern the hidden nature of man
Upon this teeming bit of solitary rock,
Moving through the void of endless flight,
From beginnings dimly sought to ends unknown?

We have clawed our way from primeval slime.
Violence and rapine the hallmarks of our kind,
But with it a shadow of tenderness scarce known:
The love of a mother for the life yet within her.

So mixed within us that hate and love are one—
Men destroy, only to build anew with love.
What half-mad monster is this we now review?
God and beast alloyed as one dark form.

Incomplete—yet seeking fulfillment in another,
Man is a compound of passions seeking life.
Wrong he may will, yet Good his inner fount—
Come we together to search the common way.

Tears and anger purify us as they fire—
Framing our humanity in a lattice-work of love.
Scan not the heavens for the true import of man;
Our commonness the spring of future excellence.

# WIFE

My love for thee is a beacon,
Now flickering in heedless wind;
Now strong with a surge of yearning
To kiss your lips most tender.

Companion of a thousand trials,
Your presence yet awakes in me
New joy that Fortune conferred
Your gentleness into my keep.

I stand—half man—and alone
If your love should fly from me.
My need for you—oft unexpressed—
Expands with each year we share.

Oh, creature of supple grace
This love from you has changed
This humble place into a home,
Alive with the melody of your soul.

Our love—that of flesh and spirit—
Entwine our hearts made human,
Sensitive to our bodily communion
Effecting *new* life to guide.

I love you for the years together,
Made holy by your touch and word.
Your hand my fount of support—
Your heart my nurture of love.

# HISTORY

History is the quest of man
To divine God's inner Plan;
Or probe the mysteries of the day
For signs of some concealed way.
If history has no comprehension,
Will man then forfeit his redemption?
Many thus have sought a sign
That history was a plan divine.
Others of less dour temper
Bid the cynics here to enter:
History is for them a sport;
Refuge for rogues of last resort.
What then may be said in her defense?
Is history purely the past tense?
History lacks not rhyme or reason,
Though her readers change by season.
When men march upon her stage,
They are hallmarks of their age.
Power is here a lasting theme;
The conqueror's recurring dream.
Caesars with their purple stride,
While their successors plotting bide.
How do we measure the economic;
A factor Marx called demonic?
Is history made by the quest for bread,
As somewhere or other I have read?
Production is a crucial base,
But no full record of the race.
Carlyle sings of the hero's role;
The deepest echo of history's soul.
Man's march is by the hero led—
As by Jesus with the fishes fed.
History is sculptured by the hero,
But before you praise, remember Nero.

History then has several factors,
Though men remain the central actors.
While boasting laws of probability,
There's room enough for capability.
The record is not full of chance,
Lest we mistake it for romance.
Law and choice are mixed as one
As each new page is deftly done.
Free will is thus a vital agent—
By Fate we are not cruelly spent.
History has her own dynamics,
Which we may master like mechanics.
It is not, however, a relentless tide,
Whose crest the Marxists aptly ride.
History then has many faces—
Of priest, king, slave and races.
Man is thus his history's maker;
Options stand for any taker.
We are then what *we* choose to be—
With no guarantees to the free.
History can but point the way;
It is up to us to join the fray.

# LIBERTY

Liberty, cleansed by the blood of patriots, is dearly won.
History resounds with the clash of arms as men conspire,
Freedom to purchase, though sacrifice all in its ardent quest—
Liberty a noble aim, for which the humblest aspire.

The poor, scarred, and insulted from the ghetto watch and hope,
A freedom to fashion, tranquil in joy, no shadow of the whip.
Loose of the oppressor's heel, standing uncowed in the sun;
Liberty transforms the heart, the wings of tyranny to clip.

Liberty invites the mind, its finest output to adduce,
To decorate the chair of freedom, the palm of Truth achieved.
Its august heart proclaim the news of probing mind—
Dim the works of man, the loss of freedom aggrieved.

Our finest hour, when men with spirit speak, unflinching—
Resolved, liberty to keep, though dear its enduring cost.
Home, kin, and land—what use when freedom dissolve?
If soul is mute, yet unchained the hand, so great the loss.

We build, labor for the day, enshrine our toil for the ages.
Liberty a sacred bond, generation to generation assign.
Liberty must grow, else stagnant become 'neath the tyrant's glance—
Deed and word its blood, hope and dream its wine.

A tender shoot, demanding the soil of heresy allowed,
Freedom, by disuse, may commonplace become, lifeless—
A dead tool of inquisitors, mean minds unyielding.
Enchained with inquiry and speech, in gilded tomb made strifeless.

Liberty is clamor, debate, and passion, precariously balanced;
Conflict of mind for Truth, pride mellowed by error.
Here no easy slumber, for freedom unguarded is erased—
The victim of neglect awaits the Black Maria of the Terror.

Duty its place, completing liberty, working for the Whole.
Here no license to action, heedless of our fellow man.
A need to work and trust, use liberty for advance of society.
Freedom with Justice to join, capping liberty with a plan.

Liberty is the nectar of men, magnifying their humanity,
Raising trite intentions—a hymn to our intellect—
A new appreciation of small ways made important—
Liberty is a due of man to man, again to collect.

# COUNTRY

Accepting of an alien swarm
From lands and tongues diverse.
Lands of cold and tropics warm—
Now round our hearths converse.

Fleeing repression's harsh embrace—
"Come make your spirits free."
Our task to build an ennobled race,
All gathered sea to sea.

At first so primitive in our ways—
The soil its fruits begrudging.
So hard the labor of those days,
As westward men were trudging.

Across the mountains and desert waste,
So pushed these fearless folk—
Calloused hand and weathered face—
The dangers to provoke.

A nation here for all to build,
Where men as equals meet.
The challenge of the gods they willed,
As men upon their feet.

A continent wide before them lay,
To bridge with ribs of steel.
Oh, high the costs along the way—
To build the commonweal.

The good folk came to make their life,
With scoundrels rich in number;
And upon the land worked man and wife,
Where now they do but slumber.

They cleared the land and made it grow,
With wheat and corn and rye;
Upon its soil, of life to sow—
Where honest men may die.

But some came slave upon these shores—
Black men of servitude,
To labor long for dandied bores,
Ere their day of rectitude.

With yet this blot upon our name,
They too must be as one;
For we must now erase the shame—
Their justice shall be won.

My country grew with sweat and toil;
Great cities did arise.
Rich was the land once barren soil—
The strength within us lies.

Made great by men of common clay
Who sought a freer clime.
Oh, search for truth, hold fast the way—
Seek justice in our time.

My country is a thing unknown—
Her truth to realize.
Long from her brow has honor shown,
Now ours to win its prize.

# COMMUNITY

There is a felt ne-ces-si-ty,
For mankind's pro-pin-qui-ty.
We surround it with pro-pri-e-ty,
And hoped-for gen-er-os-i-ty,
Then call it moral prob-i-ty
And cover it with sanc-ti-ty.
It enhances man as an en-ti-ty.
Gives rise to social pro-pen-si-ty.
Without it there is a scar-ci-ty
Of vital moral clar-i-ty.
This required pro-pin-qui-ty
Is the base of social va-lid-i-ty.
It increases human a-cu-i-ty;
Want of it creates va-cu-i-ty.
Let's work for it with a-lac-ri-ty.
Men seek it in ad-ver-si-ty;
Tyrants claim it with ver-bos-i-ty;
Their deeds deny it with ra-pid-i-ty.
Some damn it with per-vers-i-ty;
Others seek it with te-nac-i-ty.
Without it there is ca-lam-i-ty,
Which only leads to a-cer-bi-ty.
If we all have the op-por-tu-ni-ty,
It can help us grow in ma-tu-ri-ty.
It ranks in virtue with char-i-ty;
The need for shared i-den-ti-ty.

# CHURCH

The heart longs for solitude,
Quiet pause untroubled—
Promised search for Meaning
In a manner unobtrusive—
To examine the day beclouded.
Beauty is sought, examined,
Imbibed, digested, created,
As thought rushes on thought
Gaining strength, revitalized—
Crystallized in meditation.
Refined, refreshed—it grows
Nourished for coming clash.
The Spirit here resides,
Compass of the human heart.
Sympathy its pillars make;
Hope its inner strength—
Laced together by the tears
Shed by man distraught.
Church is place and intention,
A Covenant tightly bound—
Of Man and Woman exposed—
A holy need in common
Of Self to seek and fill.
Church is servant undemanding,
Minister to human wounds.
Miner for Truth concealed,
Herald of Good discovered.
The Church is born—so frail
Like Woman from our rib,
Nursed by the dreams of men—
Our errant ways improve.
Church is flesh and blood,
Living Spirit unfolding.

# THINKER

Your mind a muse, fertile and stirring,
Comprehending thought there in beauty,
Sorting fact from image blurring,
Seeking knowledge, a beloved duty.

The Thinker is act and thought combined—
Commitment to truth a vital rule,
Rejection of mystery for fact defined—
Skepticism and logic, a united tool.

For him no cloister of biased wall,
Barrier to change and factors new.
Scholasticism reject or systems fall—
Of the questioning art survive too few.

The world is complex—atom and universe,
Challenge to thought to grope and select—
Too vast in its symmetry for one poor verse—
Perish as beasts or for mind elect.

You stand unbowed by the weight involved;
The past to prune—its message impart.
Problems of Nature and society to solve,
Demanding of thought the conjurer's art.

The Thinker as artist—probing, reflecting;
Imagination his constant friend.
Let mind its way, reigning, directing—
Seeking for truth its lasting end.

Your role is vital if society to prosper,
Demean not yourself by service servile.
Shake the verities and ignorance stir—
Be true to your way and truth undefile.

# SCHOOL

My school, a chambered hall,
Sheltered nursery of learning,
Playing field for scoundrels—
Youthful prank and tome uniting.

School for some a prison,
An invitation to be truant.
A vaulted wall to scale—
Escape the discipline of books.

School for some a slum,
Crumbling plaster, disrepair—
Rambling ancient fire-traps.
Can learning ever flourish there?

School for me a way—
Romance, adventure, memories—
An arbor of ideas
And of fabled men and history.

I learned of sums and such,
What subtracted figures do compute;
That India is west of Siam—
How Pope and worldly king contest.

Friendship there was forged
By boys upon a lark.
We did the teachers try,
Their patience to provoke.

School was a testing yard,
Our childhood to consume—
So eager we for growth,
Its loss a sport become.

# BOOKS

Valiant companions of quiet times,
Your faces sweetly murmur
Of learning within systematic lines—
Echo of mind to mind.

I scan your thoughts for greatness held,
Imparted by nimble hand—
*Dear friends, sweet charmers*—
Evoking a love returned.

Hundreds of minds await my call—
Servants of my wish—
I revel in mighty learning congealed
Conferred on ages hence.

Noble civilizer of a beast,
Taming with a word.
No sword with the power of a book unleashed
Cutting, cleansing, healing.

Mighty effusion coined by the race—
Civility your gift to life.
Untilled the mind of man would lie,
If you depart our course.

# MILL

I've worked in a Mill;
I know its hidden ways—
Grime and broken windows,
Noise and petty crime.
It stands like a fortress,
Shabby and unyielding,
Stone piled on stone.
Its gates like a huge maw
Sucking in its needs,
Then spinning its web
Of finished wares—
Discharged for the world.
The Mill is a mixture
Of men and machines;
A partnership of chance,
And of silent admiration.
The machines grind away—
The men watch and wait,
They sweat and they curse,
Then step out for a butt
By the shipping room door.
A bit of lunch to sneak,
And perhaps a joke to tell.
Boys and old men—
Bloom and withered faces.
But the Mill is calling;
The machines must be fed.
It's hot and unlovely.
There's work to be done—
A job to be tended.
This is a place of heroes;
Civilization is their wars:
Matches and children's toys,
Steel and bonded paper—

Yet their fame is unknown,
Their names so commonplace.
The Mill is their life,
Their place of dignity.
They curse it like a lover
and yet defend its name.
Then their shift is over,
And out they stream home,
But first a needed beer—
So cool and rewarding.
A favorite tavern's near,
So club they together—
And rehearse their day.
There's talk of baseball,
And their last good drunk.
"My old lady's sure bitchy."
"The foreman's a nice guy,
But that Jake's a bastard."
Is this the talk of heroes—
Or of men when work is done?
They are the Heroes of the Mill,
Its flesh and its sinew—
Its heart and violence.
Their heroism is commonplace,
Yet the foundation of the race.

Some poets speak of Nature;
Others of beauty's fate.
I sing of that of the Mill.
We are part of the whole.
Eloquence is not our way.
The beauty here is hidden;
Most would never see it,
But it's with us everyday:

It's order and usefulness,
Work and needed friendship,
Laughter mixed with anger,
Products for other men
Creating joy and life.
This then is the Mill—
Family and working place,
Fraternity of the unknown,
Unending source of wisdom.

# LOVE

"Love" is a word now grown tawdry and old
By a rash exposure of its tender roots.
We debase its coinage by a rough amalgam
Of tenderness and greed, purity and pain.

Yet love remains a sentiment human,
Drawing from us a secret surrender—
Of self, ambition, station, cupidity.
By love we are never more common—nor great.

Sages and poets question love's right
To tie and bind with sanction of a kiss.
Yet lovers consent from no learning in tomes;
An inner surge of Being is enough.

Many mask love with analogy to things.
Love is not like a rose in the glen,
Nor like a rare day in May, when life's young.
It is not like a child in innocence safe.

Love is a knowledge that fullness must come
From union of flesh and spirit combined.
Love is consent to frankness and hurt,
That we might have healing of our inner self.

Love is a tension, raw and compelling—
Harshness becomes the polish of beauty.
Love is the alchemy of our vulnerable souls,
That we might read of life's completeness.

Love most of all is a transformation of Being,
Of a sensitivity so fine that for rare moments
Surrender becomes immersion of self in self—
The needs of the one, the fulfillment of the other.

# LAUGHTER

Rippling music of human soul,
Inner waters gurgling roll.
Laughter buoys, uplifting heart
Encourage this, our better part.

Humor here the noble spring
Sires laughter's joyous ring.
Tears can mark our human base,
Erase them now as useless waste.

Light the spirit, laughter made,
Lifting gloom's heavy shade,
Spreading laughter, shining coin,
Let joy the heart now purloin.

No need despair hapless sow
On sour soil sadness grow.
Laughter make the human prize,
Nurture life and joy arise.

Let life's boundless way enhance,
Christen this our better stance.
Joy, a hymn when man is whole
And laughter his defining role.

# PLEASURE

There is a term of odium,
That rivals taking opium.
Hedonism is the charge,
Damed like a criminal at large.
"Too seductive for the innocent;
"Too handy for the indulgent,"
So carp the sickly puritans,
Who would have us live like Spartans.
Pleasure her defenders name.
Must joy cower in her shame?
Recall the delicacies of the flesh,
While yet their memory is so fresh.
Savor of the cup and table,
Enjoy their boons while you are able.
Drink in the beauty of a lass,
Whose comeliness you may pass.
For man it may a science be,
To pluck the pleasures of the free.
Pleasures of the mind, says Mill,
Outrank those of heart and will.
This judgment we shall not contest;
Enjoy as many as you may wrest.
Caution is here the only rule;
Mind and body are but a tool.
All things so in moderation,
Lest mind denote its abdication.
Delights come in steady measure;
Balance each succeeding pleasure.
Man may yet be a hedonist,
While keeping Reason's loving tryst.
Need we like ascetics live
When the senses have so much to give?

Man's nature is of many parts
Appealing to the several arts.
Let Reason and the Senses win;
Their victory is for man no sin.

# HOME TOWN

My home town is a cacophony of sights and sounds
Industrial grime
Occasional crime
Sewage slime
Beers a dime
It hammers in your head the relentlessness of an industrial town
Court House crooks
Five jocks making book
Fine apartments
Dirty tenements
The bigness and grime seem to stultify by their own conformity
Wide streets
Pandering creeps
Crooked cops
Numerous wops
"Will I suffocate if I do not break the bonds that hold me in?"
Chimneys and soot
Men without roots
Stinking canal
Five bucks from a pal
Yet the very ribbons of steel and concrete are hymns all their own
Friendly faces
Civilized graces
Factories many
Bums without a penny
The smells of hotdog stands and delicatessens are a secret kind of balm
Plenty of money
Chasing the bunnies
Dirty white trash
Men with hard cash
The crowds in their sweaty profusion hold a special nearness
Lots of cars
Plenty of bars
Seventy preachers

Not enough teachers
Its richness, its color, its difference give texture to life
Broken down schools
Kids playing pool
Dagos and Honkies
Krauts like me
Boiling hot and icy cold—familiarity breeds devotion
Guys on the make
Shops selling cake
Dirty old slums
With drunken bums
We have our heroes and our weak mingled in confusion
Lots of lights
Occasional fights
People of love
Watching God above
Greeks hate Dagos, but how their kids love to intermarry
People of hate
Lying in wait
Here good men
Now and then
Plenty of problems, but guys sweating to make it go
Snobbish pride
A beautiful bride
Factories and stores
Professional whores
It's like the guy who marries the tramp and find's she a lady
Plenty of claptrap
Even a fire trap
Clear skies
Kids with bright eyes
Under her gritty crust is a heart of foul-mouth tenderness

# WAR

The steaming jungle, in lush profusion, round us grows,
Fickle weed, entangling men in unyielding grasp,
Trapping limb in a towering wall of green confusion—
Stinking death hole, vines with a viper's clasp.

Wet with rain, the tangle embroils, sodden with rot.
Overhead a scorching sun, a solar King made angry—
Conspires with the jungle web to sear the souls of men;
Great ark of fire, rolling on, by blood made hungry.

Sweat glistens, cascades from pores made raw by heat.
Flaccid figures standing watch, leached by the rain.
Guard, Oh, unholy ground, from the jungle dispossessed;
An outpost to man in the backwash of war, unlovely terrain.

This fort, a prick in the enemy's side, stands surrounded.
Earthen works raised about, a cannonade to stand.
Sharp palisades in sentinel row, the impending charge await;
Impale attacker upon their crests, disembowel the man.

We wait and watch, with straining eyes, peering for a sign,
For the foe to burst in view, weapons coughing fire;
A charge of hostile mans, these no longer men—
Running, shouting, cursing, stumbling, falling on the wire.

The jungle irrupts, hundreds rush, coming for their death.
Machine guns sputter, rifles crack, a hail of steel
Dropping men who seek our death upon this wall.
The parapet shudders from mortar shot, as bodies wheel.

The smell of battle abounds, as spent lives displace.
Men swear and cry, as death erodes their number.
Bullets whine, tearing flesh, wonder upon each face.
Steel is ordered, bayonets readied, and death her lumber.

An enemy hulk before me placed, my demise intended.
I gut him there upon that wall, small youth so fair—
Wide *his* eyes, *surprised*—transmuted to rotting waste.
The battle swirls, invading bulwark remaining there.

Ramparts drip of hopes erased and dreams asundered;
A wild confusion, twisting to evade the point—
Pressed in fearsome din, near *and yet so far*.
Redoubts made holy, a sacrament of death, with blood anoint.

Oh, ugly barter, purified in the blood so shed,
Redeemed by the hope that vain not the carnage pile;
*Something* sweeter to enhance, bought by this wager—
Mend the soul, advance, Oh, life, lest memory defile.

# THE REBEL CHARGE

## Remembrance Of An April Morning

---

Six hundred men in soldier gray
Rode out to shed their blood one day.
Their hearts a rhythm to the guns;
Oh coursing blood of Southern sons.
Their prancing steeds of restless ire
Endure the scourge of probing fire.
Mount up! Mount up! Prepare the steel.
Claim that ridge across the field.
The major on his courser flew,
While yet the grass was wet with dew.
He valiant rode—His saber high,
A vernal field on which to die.
Thundering beasts with nostrils wet,
Upon their backs were heroes set.
Their pounding hooves a song portend,
As piercing shot their bodies rend.
The horsemen rode into *that* roar;
Each called by duty to the fore.
Their sabers flashed in early morn;
Their spirits charged—so soon to mourn.
The cannons belched their ugly flame;
The searing shot the riders maim.
A Rebel yell escaped their lips—
Onrushing horde of saber tips.
A line of charging riders fall;
The cannon smoke a deadly pall.
Rank on rank the horsemen plunge,
As man and beast in dying lunge.
The saber steel and human flesh
Of gunners there it did immesh.

The Blue and Gray in tangled count,
As each new charge the Rebels mount.
The gunners work their feverish way,
As soldiers all around them lay;
Their breast carved out by cannon shot,
*So far* from home to lie and rot.
Though courage be their armor-plate,
No one can stay the hand of Fate.
Oh belching guns what pain inflict—
For *some* the end announced so quick.
So vain the charge now hasty spent,
Once brilliant ranks by bullets rent.
Their honor there upon that mound
was sealed upon that sacred ground.
The tide of Gray in valor went;
*Now* homeward were the riders bent.
Unbowed their tattered battle flags,
Though ensigns now reduced to rags.
The coursers now less speedy flew—
The day was claimed by men in Blue.
These men had wagered life and limb,
To learn the call of war is grim.
Now back in friendly land they stand
And count their losses to a man.
These Rebels then in soldier gray
Came wiser through that hellish fray.
Man and boy their valor praise—
Restive courage's fitful blaze.
May poets of another age
Frame their glory on a page.
So came the flower of the South

Risking all in the cannon's mouth.
Mourn we now their dreadful loss
Upon that deadly field to cross.
Proud we are of their fearsome ride—
Comrades *now* sleep side by side.

# GREATNESS

Two thousand years have come and gone
Since Julius Caesar's time.
His phantom legions marching on—
To Egypt or the Rhine.

With hearts of steel and flashing swords,
Across the world they stride.
These grim and weary legionnaires,
These men who have not died.

Tonight I hear their marching songs
And drum rolls as of old,
As past they come in battle dress—
A ghostly column bold.

See Heaven open up her heart
To clasp them to her breast.
Let history sing its somber ode—
For these were Caesar's best.

# DUTY

A Tribute to the Men of the *Thresher*

———————

Across the seas, wild and churning,
Sailed the Thresher, homeward yearning.
Long and low, her engines running,
No one knew that death was coming.

From the captain, young and fearless,
Came the order, swift and peerless;
To the depths they soon were plunging—
Downward groaned the *Thresher*, lunging.

The crew was tense; the ship was strained,
But the skipper knew his men were trained.
"The plates are weak," so the rumor flew,
"But who can tell," said most of the crew.

Somewhere forward a fitting wavered—
From tons of water, and nought to save her.
The bulkhead buckled, and none will know,
Save God above, why they must go.

Down to the depths—as Fate had willed,
Crashed the *Thresher*—compartments filled.
In her hull her men were dying,
Upward, Upward their cries were flying.

So still she lies on duty's errand;
Our hopes are gone and joy is barren.
But proud we are of her men of steel;
To honor the Thresher is history's seal.

As old we grow and when others ask,
Of noble deed and stalwart task,
Speak of a ship of the *Thresher* class,
For glory is hers—from first to last.

# BATTLE

Under a jungle canopy of green,
Toiled a company of weary Marines.
Hunter and hunted for an enemy unseen,
Hidden deep in a tangle screen.

Long the patrol and yet no fight—
All the day and half the night,
Searching, seeking, looking, waiting,
Half in dread the carnage hating.

These are the men of Company "B,"
Longing for homes across the sea.
Beardless youths and hardened man
That a sense of duty here did send.

A hapless people to protect,
Lest by omission their freedom wreck,
So deck these lads with arms of war
And inure them to the cannon's roar.

Jungle, jungle—God, so thick!
Ten of the men with fever sick.
Keep your weapon by your side—
Wade the river deep and wide.

Labor under that hellish sun,
To take some ground and keep it won.
"Keep watch! The enemy is near,"
Says the Captain. "Show no fear."

From the foliage full of rot
May soon come the killing shot.
Fate may yet still have her way—
Some of us will die today.

Though our numbers are so few,
Each must now his duty do.
Fight the fight—see it through;
Cross the river two by two.

Now their volleys soon erupt.
Can this but mortal flesh corrupt?
So clever in their ambuscade—
The Captain makes the call for aid.

Five to one—the odds must be,
Firing at us from ground and tree.
Machine guns spew their deadly steel;
Dead men fall-What did they feel?

"Ammo, ammo, pass it here."
"Look for targets"—"Guard the rear;"
"Watch for movement—fire fast,
If you don't, we will not last."

The Captain falls with a bloody wound;
He groans and turns and dies so soon.
No time for that—must fire back,
As bodies round us death doth stack.

Of them, we take a goodly toll;
They die up yonder on that knoll.
Howe'er the fight, we wage it well,
Though now we know of earthly hell.

How long can human soul endure,
These deadly scourgings to inure?
The question did within me stir,
As sweat and blood my vision blur.

My senses numbed by shot and shell;
I shot a man and there he fell.
But more came on for hand-to-hand,
And now we matched them man to man.

The cold steel broke on rib and bone.
They came together and died alone.
We stood our ground and held them back,
Though red the earth at first so black.

At last the foe no longer came,
But only God's cool, soothing rain.
Our bodies pained—our ammo spent,
And with its end our spirits rent.

Of this there is no more to tell,
Save only that boys may die so well.
So many came with the flower of youth
To harvest courage's costly fruit.

# WANDERER

Yours is not the hearth side,
Nor a place called home.
Look you toward the open road;
All the world to roam.

Never think of times gone by—
Never turn and say,
I'll come back my true love,
In some other day.

When the sea is pounding fiercely,
A call to kindred hearts,
Then rouse yourself from slumber
To ship to unknown parts.

Turn your face toward the cooling wind,
Let not your spirit wane.
The gypsy's call is in your blood,
Like good red wine from Spain.

But, Oh, what cost the vagrant's life,
And the free-booter's way,
For no one has you in her heart
To think of through the day.

Each new road you wander by,
Each new place you see—
Carry you back ten thousand miles,
Where your heart would rather be.

Years will pass, my wandering soul,
Till it is time for rest.
Long you'll wonder what might've been;
Long will you look to the west.

Here is a word to adventurers young—
Never thirst for foreign place.
Find yourself a willowy lass,
And kiss her gentle face.

Envy you not the voyager's call,
Nor a far-distant strand,
Else many a year you'll wander by—
In the Legion of the Damned.

# HELL

I've been beyond the gates of Hell;
I know its worst ordeal.
Your soul shall never enter here—
As long as there is hope.

For we who march among the dead
Have died a thousand times.
Our bodies walk the paths of life,
But here our spirits cry.

We know the coldness of the tomb
And life's so silent way,
Where everyday's a Hell on earth;
When forgotten is our name.

We curse the stars that let us be
In the living death of life;
There is no balm to soothe our souls—
The men whom God forgot.

# SUICIDE

I've a meeting in the valley of Death
At some appointed hour,
And I shall keep my rendezvous
Before the dawn shall rise.
And time and space deter me not,
For I will travel far
To woo the cold and beautiful,
My dark Angel of Death.

# MARTYRDOM

### On the Fiftieth Anniversary
### of the Easter Uprising In Dublin

---

When the ensigns of empire are unfurled no more,
The lessons etched with their rifle shot
Will throb the pulse and awaken the heart
Of free men all clothed in majesty.

Long lay Ireland under alien scorn,
Hammered by batteries of hate and neglect,
Crushing her spirit and denying her name.
Ireland groaned while her children wept.

Patriots dreamed of a commonwealth free.
Were these but phantoms never to be—
Of soil and kindred blood reaching the sea—
Joined at last in the furnace of unity?

The miners and sappers of reaction's guard,
Cutting and blasting at Ireland's pride.
The Irish Constabulary crippling the land,
Wounding the soul of her suffering folk.

"The time has come," vowed Irish lads,
"To spill our blood in her defense."
"Rise up! Rise up!" the poets sang,
"Lest new generations mark our shame."

So drilled these stout lads of the I. R. A.
On rain-swept fields near Dublin Town.
Across the green land their trumpet call—
"Oh, men of Ireland, come set her free."

Connolly, Clarke, MacDonagh, MacNeill,
These were the rebels of Irish steel—
Plotters by night—heroes by day—
Arms from the West, by way of Tralee.

"Hurry, man, hurry—the order's been given.
'Tis the day after Easter—the fuse has been lit."
The Volunteers march out in Wexford and Cork—
Hearts pounding fiercely for Ireland redeemed.

Avenge they now their desolate people—
The Dublin Brigade, the Hibernian Rifles.
In a Republic of Blood they'll soon be elected—
A stand to be made—a world resurrected.

"Ireland, Ireland, at last you'll be free,
Capture the strong points, de Valera, Daly."
"Quickly, quickly, the time's running out."
"The English are coming with cannon aplenty."

The fighting is bitter; the casualties, many—
From house to house the enemy creeps,
Watching for snipers—clearing the way—
Dublin Fusiliers and Sherwood Foresters.

In skirmish line, with bayonets ready—
The English advance in a storm of steel.
Outpost by outpost, the rebels are taken,
Though many fall—their life's blood committed.

The city is torn, twisted, and gutted.
English artillery has pocked it for history.
Resist day by day, these stout sons of Ireland,
Though hopeless now their cause become.

With all the world watching, their numbers diminish.
A patriot's death their only known marker.
At last they surrender, undaunted—defiant,
Yet Ireland was served by their valiant encounter,

Now treated like dogs, these flowers of Erin—
Imprisoned, defiled, condemned without mercy.
Their sentence is swift, the bullets unerring.
England is served and martyrs engendered.

Yet Ireland remembers their selfless adventure.
A handful of men with their courage as armor,
An alien host, their empire to challenge—
For the freedom to live and the peace to die.

The lesson learned in the streets of Dublin
Is larger than Ireland—a Writ for the World,
That man, may he suffer, longs to be free—
For courage and daring, the coin of liberty.

# SACRIFICE

If we should die tonight,
In some forgotten fight,
Think not it was in vain—
This carnage and its pain.

Ours was the cup of life—
Hearth, children, and wife—
Spent now in innocence,
Hushed ever in reticence.

With our lives we now do seal
Upon this death-scarred battle field:
Liberty was our holy trust—
Protect it till our weapons rust.

How long, we ask, can men be free,
When tyranny is allowed to be,
Grinding humanity in its wake,
As all men its slaves doth make?

Hold high the banner of liberty;
The human heart in sanctity.
Came we to this tropic place,
To shed our blood for another race.

Call us not by a hero's name,
We who fall by shell and flame.
When time has writ its last "amen,"
Remember only that we were men.

# PEACE

## Memories of a Spring Morning After Appomattox

---

The cannonade is silent;
The drums roll no more.
We speak in muffled whisper
Of the dread cause of war.

We gather all this morning
To see the men disband.
They were a mighty legion
Of a mighty, mighty land.

Four years of bloody struggle
To set the black man free.
The armies clashed together.
Would reunion ever be?

From Gettysburg to Shiloh,
The muskets, how they rang.
Remember—O, the grapeshot,
As through the ranks it sang.

Now we stand altogether,
Upon this sacred field.
Mourn our fallen comrades—
They were the Union's shield.

At last the war is over—
Past the hate and despair.
Let us bind up all our brothers,
And the Union now repair.

# PAIN

A stab of pain awakes to life
Memories buried of an animal past.
We start, whine—nerves all alive,
Fly from me, O dreadful thing.

No ancient beast in jungle wood
With speed recoils to piercing barb
As Man—that half-digested child—
The dirk of pain evades in haste.

Pain—the Mark of Cain—pervades
Fiber and muscle, Being enveloped,
Sensitivity dilated and sharp;
Pain—with Pleasure—a dyad for man.

Inherent by Nature in flesh made vital,
Signal unique that ill approaches.
Watchman, Friend—vigilance profound,
Protect from harm yet hurt inflict.

Courage required when an audience imposed
By Pain—sovereign, willful, demanding.
Man is fortified, growing in stature,
Bending his knee not in subjection.

Science progresses, this dragon to slay,
Bit by bit his domain to acquire,
Reducing pain to a lesser dimension,
Enhancing humanity, releasing strength.

Pain yet remains useful in surrender.
*What* temper the Will if pain resolve?
If threat remove, *what* value the prize?
Man is not strong by indulgence made.

Man is a hero when pain encountered,
Not if he meets it with Stoic acceptance,
But if he cry, falter, and tremble—
Yet carry on, *resolve* unaltered.

# LONELINESS

Upon a busy highway
Today I chanced to meet
A wizened little wanderer,
Searching for *his* dream.
Dirt and grime his raiment—
His suit of tatters made.
The figure stooping slightly,
His walk a shuffling gait.
He had a weathered face—
A mask for hidden thoughts,
Lined as a spider's web—
It told of passage made:
Of flight from place forgot,
Escape to goal unknown.
I looked within those eyes;
The message made me weep.
Hollows of sadness and woe
Bespoke of wife and child,
Of happier days at home
Now erased by time's lament.
Upon those shoulders hunched
He carried a burden of tears.
Loneliness his only plan—
More past than future left.
His is the mark of the hunted,
Cursed by memories dimming.
Laughter no longer his way;
The miles have made him forget.
The wanderer's a dead man,
Rotting from within.

An ebbing speck of humanity
That chanced one time to be.
Compact us here this moment—
Let no more so be lost!

# GRIEF

## A Child's Remembrance

---

Can we but know the love so widely shared,
For one so young and lively to our glance.
Her youth—our own lost pledge of innocence.
Her life, now spent, a link of heart to heart.

Ours is a gladder time that she did live,
Though pale the solace of our sorrow's bond.
So short a time to list her in our midst,
Yet her short life gives fullness to our own.

A child is seed—time, growth, and harvest, all;
The richness there if we but pause to reap.
This is a loss more cutting than a sword,
Yet may we learn of life in her sweet ebb.

# EVIL

## The Left Hand of God

---

What doth preside upon that side,
Hidden most from view,
Of God in beauty and splendor enthroned,
The quarter but known to few?
The left side of God is thus enclosed
In darkness made abstruse.
Sorcerers claim that *there* iniquity
Upon man has been let loose.
Magnificence adorns his <u>other</u> wing;
Righteousness doth prevail.
Salvation's *there* in glory enshrined,
Justice in purity's mail.
Freedom, honesty, and virtue impaled,
Hang there upon a nail;
Earned by the pain of the Prince of men,
Born of a woman's travail.
All things creditable are so inscribed,
Of a spring transcendental.
The acts of men are alleged to pale—
*Our* good but incidental.
If this be so, as the prophets allege,
The left side is also God's.
Prince of Darkness, *His* servant too—
Sin and the scourging rods.
What evils plague this earthly place,
Are then by God's hand set.
Man is no more than result of the times,
Of the froth of the sea still wet.
Man *must* stand, *Maker* or *made*
Of this pale environment.

He, the *Ruler* and *subject* himself,
Or nought but divine sediment.
If such admonitions are then disallowed,
And man is not made free,
What then the intention of this God,
Who sits above, one in three?
With freedom denied and man enchained
By oath of high authority,
What course remains, but to ascribe
Our woes to calm divinity?
The dextral side in glory shines—
A holy vision beatific—
Soul of love, ennobling all,
With nature quite pacific.
The other arm must then endure
Our full note of odium.
God must then the burden bear—
Love and hate to sum.
Freedom and duty and their weight,
With man must thus devolve,
Else God in His march, corruption explain,
And *Himself* now absolve.

# DEATH

Death came to me one night,
In a vision cold and clear.
White was its nocturnal gown,
Not black of mourning set.
The figure, tall and slim—
Still, but for the wind.
Soon beckoned with her hand—
A tool of flesh and blood,
*Not* clammy bones unfurled.
Her face a wisp of beauty
Seemed *almost* as if to smile.
I yearned to sense her touch—
A willowy body so supple.
Was this the Death bespoke
By hoary hags of yore,
A maiden made of ash—
Whose call a boon most feared?
The vision now did fade;
I woke from sleep direct.
The thoughts within that view
Now mine to reconstruct.
Her stance was not unnatural;
Her name *in time* be known.
It is of Nature's provision,
That she at last should come
And woo her Sister's lover,
On pathways yet discover.
Her Sister is of life;
We love and seek the other.
Life is the maiden's call—
Expected thing perceived,
While Death her counterpart;
Embrace it warmly when
It chance to be our lot

To tread her way unknown.
Death is for man a part
Of life and love expressed.
Seek not her hidden home;
Her hand you cannot stay.
We fear her unknown touch—
Life loves us far too much.
The mists conceal her goal
And terror consumes our heart;
Man, Oh, Man, you quail
And tremble before this lass.
Remember my vision clear,
Of Death it did divine.
Live *now* the moment's fire—
Thirst for its fullest depth;
But soon you will consume
The measured desire of life.
Then await the Sister of Death,
Her siren song to sing—
Of magic now disguised—
This earth a *little* place—
Death your porter shall be
To knowledge now withheld.
Her estate beyond the gate
Is darkness' richest hour.
I am a fool to speak,
My learning to instruct.
The domain of Death is real;
Our conscious Self submerge
Within its endless dream—
For Time and Space annul.
Immerse your total Self—
Enjoy its timeless stream,
And *sense-less* order learn.

Printed in the United States
By Bookmasters